ZEN

MADE EASY

D1022770

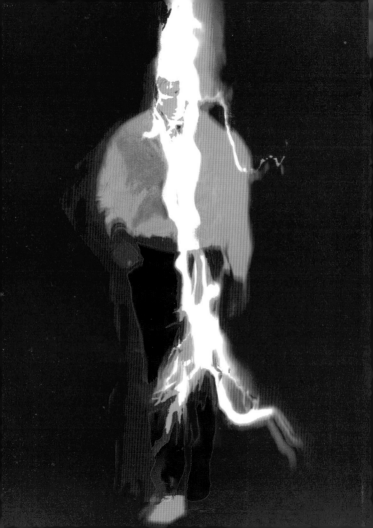

ZEN

MADE EASY

Timothy Freke

GODSFIELD PRESS

Library of Congress
Cataloging-in-Publication Data Available

10 9 8 7 6 5 4 3 2 1

Published in 1999 by
Sterling Publishing Company, Inc.
387 Park Avenue South,
New York, N.Y. 10016
© 1999 Godsfield Press
Text © 1999 Timothy Freke

Timothy Freke asserts the moral right to be
identified as the author of this work.

Distributed in Canada by Sterling Publishing
c/o Canadian Manda Group,
One Atlantic Avenue, Suite 105,
Toronto, Ontario, Canada M6K 3E7
Distributed in Australia by
Capricorn Link (Australia) Pty Ltd
P O. Box 6651, Baulkham Hills
Business Centre, NSW 2153, Australia

All rights reserved.

Every effort has been made to ensure that
all the information in this book is accurate.
However, due to differing conditions, tools,
and individual skills, the publisher cannot be
responsible for any injuries, losses, and other
damages which may result from the use of
the information in this book.

Printed and bound in Hong Kong

Sterling ISBN 0-8069-9921-7

Library of Congress Cataloging-in-Publication Data
Freke, Timothy. 1959-
    Zen made easy : an introduction to the basics of the
ancient art of Zen / Timothy Freke.
        p.   cm.
    Includes index.
    ISBN 0-8069-9921-7
    1. Zen Buddhism---Quotations, maxims, etc.   I. Title.
BQ9267.F744   1999
294.3'927--DC21
                                        99-20712
                                            CIP

ACKNOWLEDGMENTS
*The publishers wish to thank the following
for the use of pictures:*
Bridgeman Art Library: 31, 37, 46, 53a, 54
Bruce Coleman Collection:
7, 22, 31, 43, 47, 51, 65, 68
Circa Photo Library/Tjalling Halbertsma:
17, 52–53, 67
Circa Photo Library/Barrie Searle: 61
Eye Ubiquitous/Neil Berry: 25
Eye Ubiquitous/Paul Thompson: 14b
Eye Ubiquitous/Yiorgos Nikiteas: 48–49
Hutchison Library/Patricio Goycoolea:
6, 26, 34–35, 38–39, 60, 62, 70, 74
Images: 45
Mary Evans Picture Library:
38b, 56a, 56–57
Tony Stone Images:
9, 36–37, 50, 59, 63, 64, 66, 76–77
(a = *above*; b = *below*)

Illustration:
Lorraine Harrison, Ivan Hissey

Photography:
Ian Parsons

Contents

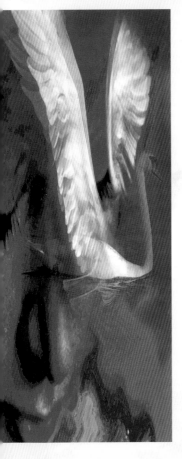

Introduction: Zen Made Easy?

Zen is easy. Nothing could be easier. Zen is life exactly as it is. Here and now. The same joys and sufferings.

The same daily needs. No clever ideas about anything. Nothing supernatural or out of the ordinary. No difference from what you are experiencing right at this moment. Except one, that is. No "you."

Above: A drum and stick from a Zen Buddhist monastery in Japan.

Zen is a Japanese name for the ancient and perennial mystical philosophy of Oneness, at the heart of which is the understanding that we do not exist as separate persons but coexist with all that is in an indivisible unity. Seemingly separate beings such as "you" and "I" are actually like waves rising and falling on one great eternal sea of Being.

The Great Way is easy
for those who have no preferences.

Sengs'tan

Above: **At the heart
of Zen is a sense
that we are all part of
something greater,
just as each wave is
part of the ocean.**

The Web of Life

> "People are scared to empty their minds fearing
> that they will be engulfed by the void.
> What they don't realize is that their own mind
> is the void. "
>
> *Huang-po*

Everything in life is part of an interdependent whole. Without me writing there could not be you reading. Without daily food there would be no me to write. Without the sun there would be no food. Without all the fundamental forces of the universe there would be no sun. Through a vast web of connections everything is linked to everything else. Separate things only exist in relationship to the Whole. In themselves they have no independent existence. We experience things as separate because we think of them as separate. But when the mind is still, reality is experienced as empty of all separateness. No me. No you. No anything. This is Zen.

All life is changing, all the forms of it, and we flow with the river or we refuse. If we flow with the river, we can digest it, as it were, as we flow, and feel no suffering. Accept it and we are one with it; resist it and we are hurt.

Christmas Humphreys

Below: Zen Buddhist gardens are designed with meditation and contemplation in mind.

Zen and Now

A special transmission
    outside the scriptures.
No dependence upon words
    and concepts.
Direct pointing to the heart
    of man.
Seeing into one's own nature.

Bodhidharma

In the fifth century B.C.E. an Indian
sage known as the Buddha restated
the perennial mystical philosophy
in his own distinctive way and
inadvertently created a religion.
In the sixth century C.E. an
enlightened follower of
his teachings journeyed
from India to China. He
was named "Bodhid-
harma" or "Knower of
the Way."

Left: **A statue of
the Buddha from
Sukothai, Thailand.**

ENLIGHTENMENT NOT RELIGION

Buddhism was already established in China as a religion, and the emperor regarded himself as a devout Buddhist. Bodhidharma, however, brought something more than religion; he brought the unique perceptions of an enlightened mind. Despite this, or perhaps because of this, he made little impression. He confused and angered the Chinese emperor and found only one student capable of receiving the transmission of enlightenment.

Left and right:
Pictures and statues of the Buddha give the impression that the Buddha is someone "outside." But the Buddha in Zen represents the essential nature "inside" each and every one of us.

BUDDHISM + TAOISM = ZEN

Although in their own lifetimes Bodhidharma and his disciple Hui-ke would have appeared as little more than no-good "dharma bums," they are the roots of Zen. They inspired a lineage of enlightened masters who fused Bodhidharma's uncompromisingly experiential Buddhism with indigenous Chinese Taoism. This created a vibrant and anarchic approach to spirituality known as "Ch'an." In the twelfth century, Ch'an reached Japan where it acquired the familiar name "Zen."

Above: Buddhism and Taoism were combined to create Zen.

ZEN HAS NO HISTORY

Zen Buddhism is simply a particular approach to spirituality, molded by the cultures from which it evolved. It must not be confused with the Zen experience. Bodhidharma did not bring Zen to China. Zen was already there. Zen is the natural state of things unclouded by the illusion of separateness. Zen has no history. It is always here and now.

Right: Buddhism was brought to China by Bodhidharma. It was fused with Taoism to create "Ch'an" — in Japan this became Zen.

BEIJING

TOKYO

KYOTO

SEOUL

KAMAKURA

OSAKA

XI'AN

Who Is Reading This?

> Only by accepting that the ego is a fabricated
> illusion do we walk the Buddha's Way.
>
> *Dogen*

The Zen masters are not interested in expounding a system of teachings, but in helping their students discover who they are. Master Bassui reduced the whole of Zen teachings to one phrase: "Seeing one's own nature is Buddhahood." When asked how to actually see into one's own nature, Bassui would reply, "Now! Who is asking?"

WE ARE NOT WHO WE THINK WE ARE

Zen teaches that anything we think we are is just a thought in the mind. We are not the thought. We are the consciousness that witnesses the thought. But even to say this is just another thought! No wonder when the emperor asked of Bodhidharma, "Who are you?" the Zen master replied, "I have no idea." Zen teaches that we must go beyond any conceptualization of who we are and be what we are.

Left: **A statue of Diabutsu – the Great Buddha – from Kamakura, Japan.**

made
easy

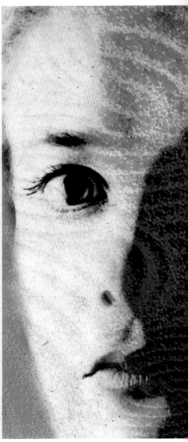

The big mind in which we must
have confidence is not something
you can experience objectively.
It is something that is always with
you, always on your side. Your eyes
are on your side, for you cannot see
your eyes, and your eyes cannot see
themselves. Eyes only see things
outside, objective things. If you
reflect on your self, that self is not
your true self anymore. You cannot
project yourself as an objective thing
to think about. The mind that is
always on your side is not just your
mind, it is universal mind, always
the same, not different from
another's mind. It is Zen mind.
It is big, big mind.

Shunryu Suzuki

What are you?

What is there in the entire universe
that is not you?

Guangfan

BUDDHA-NATURE

Our ideas about who we are construct for us a false self or ego. When these ideas are absent, however, we can directly experience our deeper Buddha-nature, which the modern master Shunryu Suzuki called "Big Mind" or "Zen Mind." This universal Consciousness that animates all of life is our true identity.

Left: **Buddha-nature is the shared, universal Consciousness within all of us.**

Above: Part of a shrine in the Tai Shan
Taoist mountain. Zen encourages an expansive
perspective of the world around us.

FIND OUT NOW!

However much you try to find yourself through logical reasoning
and definition, you are doomed to failure. Even if you search the core
of your being, becoming full of questioning, you won't find anything
that you could call a personal mind or essence. Yet when someone
calls your name, something in you hears and responds. Find out who
it is! Find out now! The dilemmas of birth and death are huge and
time is passing. Make the most of it. It won't wait for you.

Bassui

No One Is Enlightened

> Delusion is not being aware of
> your fundamental mind.
> Enlightenment is realizing your
> fundamental essence.
>
> *Mazu*

Enlightenment is the spontaneous recognition that there has never been any such thing as a "you" or a "me." Instead, there is only the unfolding of Buddha-nature. The persistent idea of being a "me" obscures our true impersonal identity. The illusionary separate self is no more than a passing cloud traversing the great open sky of our deeper being.

WHO WANTS TO REALIZE ZEN?

Student *"What is Zen?"*

Master *"It is right before your eyes."*

Student *"So why can't I see it?"*

Master *"Because you have a 'me.'"*

Student *"If I no longer have the concept 'me,' will I realize Zen?"*

Master *"If there is no 'me' who wants to realize Zen?"*

Left: Buddha-nature unfolds like a flower opening to the sun. This golden Buddha is from Western Honshu, Japan.

Above: **Zen is understanding that the separate self is an illusion.**

A PARADOXICAL PREDICAMENT

Zen teachings on enlightenment present us with a profound paradox: the enlightened master is someone who knows he or she is not a "someone." To become enlightened is not to gain something wonderful. It is to lose something. It is finally abandoning the illusionary idea of being a separate self and discovering the wonder that has been our true nature all along.

NOTHING IN IT FOR "ME"

The Zen Path takes us on a journey, the destination of which is the realization that there never was anyone to make the journey. Enlightenment is not something that benefits "you" or "me." It is the absence of the illusion of there being a "you" or "me" to benefit. Enlightenment is held up as the

ultimate goal of Buddhism, but ironically it is only when the concept of being a "someone" who could achieve anything is abandoned that enlightenment naturally occurs.

Above: This painting by Utagawa Kuniyoshi depicts the Sumikida River embankment beneath Mount Fuji.

The experience is not the goal of Zen endeavor, for the will to achieve defeats itself.

Christmas Humphreys

A NATURAL PROCESS

Enlightenment is something that just happens. It is an impersonal natural occurrence. Just as flowers bloom and the sun sets, some human beings awaken. Praising someone who is enlightened and condemning ourselves for our ignorance is therefore as foolish as approving of the bloom but denouncing the bud.

Below: **Enlightenment happens when the time is right – as naturally as when the sun sets.**

GOING HOME

Although enlightenment may sound like a strange and supernatural state, Zen teaches that it is actually utterly familiar – like going home. Master Foyan compares it to suddenly seeing your father after many years of absence. You know who it is without any doubt whatsoever. You don't need to ask anyone else. Enlightenment is like this. Enlightenment that needs to be certified by some authority is not true enlightenment.

Enlightenment is
beyond concepts.
No one has ever attained it.

Ying-an

Above: **The wondrous beauty of
nature reflects the unfathomable
concept of enlightenment.**

Mind, clear of all limitations.
Confusion is replaced by serenity.
Ideas of holiness are irrelevant.
He is not enlightened,
but he is not unenlightened.
When there is no duality,
a thousand eyes
could not see any division.
Even if birds dropped flowers
where he walked,
all praise would be without
     meaning.

Kuo-an Shih-yuan

The Road to Nowhere

**When everything is seen as One,
we return to the Source
and stay where we have always been.**

Seng-t'san

Zen, like all forms of Buddhism, essentially teaches that the path to transcending the ego-self is through stilling the mind and opening up the heart. Meditation clears the mind of its contents and allows us to become aware of Consciousness itself – Big Mind. Nurturing loving kindness unites us with other beings and undermines and diminishes our habitual self-orientation.

GETTING TO WHERE YOU ARE

But Zen is not about getting anywhere. Zen is uncovering what is already there. Enlightenment is not becoming anything. Enlightenment is being what you already are.

Right: **Meditation helps to empty the mind so that we can become aware of Consciousness itself.**

Our Buddha-nature is there from the
    very beginning.
It is like the sun emerging from
    behind clouds.
It is like a mirror which reflects
    perfectly
when it is wiped clean and returned to
    its original clarity.

Ho-shan

THE GRADUAL PATH

There are two approaches to Zen, sometimes known as the Gradual Path and the Abrupt Path. The Gradual Path emphasizes patient perseverance in the practice of Zen principles and the progressive wiping clean from the mirror of the mind the illusion of separate individuality. In this way the conditions conducive to enlightenment are created.

A sudden clash of thunder,
the mind-doors burst open,
and lo, there sits old man
Buddha-nature in all his
homeliness.

Chao-pien

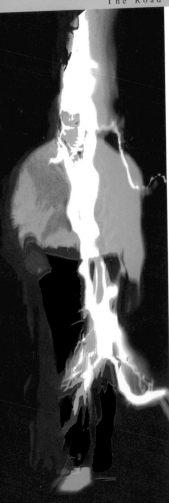

THE ABRUPT PATH

The Abrupt Path is sometimes known as "The Diamond Thunderbolt." It emphasizes the sudden and involuntary nature of spiritual awakening. It teaches that if we strive to awaken gradually we are in danger of only endorsing the illusion of being a "doer" – an autonomous individual. The Abrupt Path encourages us to go directly to the very foundation of the problem and uproot the illusion of separateness immediately through an instantaneous burst of intuitive insight.

> **Understand the Abrupt**
> **Doctrine**
> **and external disciplines are**
> **unnecessary.**
>
> *Hui-neng*

Left: Monks follow a path through the snow. Zen offers two ways toward enlightenment: the Gradual Path and the Abrupt Path.

Ah, This!

Don't search for truth.
Just stop having opinions.

Sengt'san

Zen is not about grasping certain ideas. It is about discovering the source of all ideas. It is not about comprehending convoluted philosophical theories. It is about intuitive insight. As Master Daie explained: "The teachings expounded in the Buddhist scriptures are merely commentaries on the spontaneous cry – 'Ah, this!'"

Confused by thoughts,
we experience duality
in life. Unencumbered
by ideas, the enlightened
see the one Reality.

Hui-neng

ZEN OPINIONS

Zen teachings are thoughts that seek to bring our attention to the essence of Mind. But this is not revealed by ideas, but by their absence. All ideas and opinions, even Zen opinions, clutter up consciousness and distract us from an awareness of awareness itself. Silence cannot be experienced as long as we keep saying the word "silence." Zen Mind cannot be experienced as long as we fill it with Zen thoughts.

Left: **Zen thoughts do not lead to Zen mind, because all ideas and opinions clutter the clarity of pure consciousness.**

A FINGER POINTING AT THE MOON

Zen is not a religious doctrine passed from generation to generation. It is a living experience of life itself of which the traditional teachings are a faint echo. Zen teachings are often compared to a finger pointing at the moon. The finger is not the moon, and the teachings are not Zen. They gesture toward something ineffable and ultimately completely incommunicable. To see the moon it is necessary to stop looking at the pointing finger. Likewise, Zen teachings are only finally understood when they are abandoned.

Zen teachings have been likened to a finger pointing toward the moon — to see the moon you must stop looking at the finger.

ZEN TEACHES NOTHING

Zen teaches nothing. Whatever teachings there
are in Zen, they come out of one's own mind.
We teach ourselves; Zen merely points the way.

D.T. Suzuki

NO IDEA

*An arrogant student who felt he
had achieved emptiness of mind
boasted to his master, "Now I have
no idea." The master replied, "Why
stagger about under the weight of
this concept 'no idea'?"*

When the curious ask
    you what It is,
Don't affirm or deny anything.
Anything affirmed or denied
    is not true,
How can someone say what It is
When he has not fully known It?
And, knowing, what letters can
    be sent
From lands where words find no
    road to travel?
To their questions, therefore,
    offer silence.
Only silence and a pointing finger.

Zen Poem

ZEN IS ...

Zen masters are trying to free their students from whatever concepts they happen to be trapped in. If they are caught up in a conventional view of the world, the master may introduce philosophical reasoning to undermine and challenge their belief in concrete reality. If, however, they are caught up in an abstract intellectual understanding of life and believe everything to be unreal, the master may simply hit them hard on the head with his old stick. Zen is neither this or that. It is What-is with no ideas about it.

HEALING THE SICKNESS
OF SEPARATENESS

All verbal teachings are just to
cure an illness. Different illnesses
require different cures. If the
cure works, the teachings are true.
If they don't, the teachings are
false. True teachings are false if they
create opinions. False teachings
are true if they destroy delusions.
The illness is an illusion
anyway, so all the cures are
also illusions.

Baizhang

Right: It is a common
practice for Zen monks
to use *Kyosaku* sticks
to aid meditation.

Get Real!

> The truth is
> to be lived not mouthed.
>
> *Hui-neng*

Zen is not interested in abstract metaphysical speculations. Zen wants us to "get real!" To really be alive. To really know who we are. To really see things as they are. When students get lost in Zen theories, the masters are compassionately merciless in bringing them down to earth.

SOMETHING FROM NOTHING?

Hoping to show off his understanding of Buddhist philosophy, a young student announced to Master Dokuon, "In reality nothing exists. There is no enlightenment and no delusion, no wise man and no average man. There is no giving, and nothing is receiving." Dokuon sat silently smoking, ignoring the pupil who became increasingly

agitated. Suddenly Dokuon whacked the student hard with his bamboo pipe, making him yell with anger. "If nothing exists," inquired the master, "where did this anger come from?"

Below: The Zen master stands behind his students with a *Kyosaku* stick — he taps their shoulders during meditation.

DRUNKS OR MONKS – BUT NOT PRIESTS!

Having lived the life of an eccentric tramp for most of his days, Master Ikkyu became an abbot of an important Zen temple. Just before his death he foretold that some of his students would become meditative hermits in the mountains, while others would drink wine and frequent brothels. He himself had followed both of these ways and he regarded either as good Zen. His only wish was that none of them became professional Zen priests, babbling on about Buddhism. This would be anti-Zen.

DON'T BE A BLOCKHEAD

Right: The fluid lines of a Zen garden help Zen practitioners develop a serene mind.

Master Hogen said to a monk, "Look at this big stone. Do you think it is inside or outside your mind?" The monk replied, "According to Buddhist teachings, everything is a projection of the mind, so I conclude that it is inside my mind." Hogen commented, "Don't you get tired carrying around such a heavy stone?"

made
easy

Above:
This sixteenth-
century print
celebrates the
natural beauty
of Japan.

Buddha-babble

**Buddha-babble
blocks the Way.**

Ikkyu

Nothing gets in the way of the Zen experience as much as Zen prattle. Zen demands we live authentically, without indulging in unnecessary spiritual chatter. Master Fenyang teaches, "When you are deluded even a thousand scriptures are not enough. When you understand, even one word is too much."

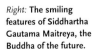
Right: **The smiling features of Siddhartha Gautama Maitreya, the Buddha of the future.**

RAT DROPPINGS STEW
A Zen master refused to say a word about Zen. One of his students complained, "This is a waste of time. I don't

expect a complete exposition of Buddhism, but at least to hear two words – 'Absolute Truth.'" The master retorted,"There is not a single word to say about 'Absolute Truth.'" As soon as he said this he frowned and announced, "It was pointless to say that." In an adjoining room another master overheard this conversation and commented, "A fine pot of stew befouled by two rat droppings."

Above: **Zen gardens favor symmetry and simplicity in order to encourage meditation and a still mind.**

The Magic of the Moment

> Moment after moment,
> everything comes out of nothingness.
> This is the true joy of life.
>
> *Shunryu Suzuki*

The Zen Path is a circle that brings us right back to where we already are – here and now. This moment is the only reality. The past and future are abstractions. This is what is. Enlightenment happens right now or not at all. When we penetrate the present it becomes a doorway to eternity.

THE MIRACLE OF EXISTENCE

The whole mystery is present in this instant; not in its particular qualities and characteristics, but in the fact that it is at all. Zen is to

Right: **If we follow the Zen Path we will return to where we started – here and now.**

be aware of the miracle of existence. It is to enter utterly into the ever-changing richness of experience, to dive into the fullness of the senses, unrestrained by the thinking mind.

**Here it is — right now.
Start thinking about it
and you miss it.**

Huang-po

ENTERING IN

When a student asked to be shown the way to enlightenment, the master replied, "Do you hear that babbling brook? Enter there." Zen is taking time actually to see and hear and feel. Zen is dissolving the self into the moment and ignoring the future. When a student asked Master T'sui-wei, "What is the essence of Buddhism?" the Master whispered, "Look how high these bamboos are! And how short those over there!"

Above: **Zen is a puzzle which leads you to the center**

AN AWARENESS OF WONDER

When a student asked Master Rugan, "What is your Buddhism?" he replied, "Piling fresh fruit in a basket without a bottom." The way of Zen is to embrace the abundant experiences life offers and to enjoy them in the moment while they are still fresh. Then to hold on to nothing, but to let the present become the past, confident that the basket will continue to be filled with new extraordinary fruit as life constantly unfolds its mysteries.

The Wordless Sutra

The scripture in
which all the Buddha's
teachings may be
found is continually
being recited.

Wensui

When a student asked Master Yunmen, "What is Buddhism?" he replied, "Dried dung." Zen is not about developing a rarefied "spiritual" approach to life. It is about penetrating the mystery that permeates the whole of existence, from the glory of the distant stars to excrement under our feet.

Zen opens a man's eyes to the greatest mystery as it is daily and hourly performed.

D. T. Suzuki

LISTEN TO THE CALL OF FROGS

To benefit from reading the sutras you must first awaken the mind that reads them. The wonderful nature of your mind, unchanging through countless ages, is the essence of all the sutras. To understand this essence, listen to the call of frogs, the billowing wind, the falling rain, all speaking the wonderful language of the Essential Nature. If you hear the wordless sutra once, the heavens will become sutras filled with golden words, clear and obvious before you.

Master Bassui

HAIKU

Master Ikkyu advised that instead of endlessly chanting sutras, Zen students should learn to read the love letters sent by the snow, the wind, and the rain. Zen poets did just this and developed a form of poetry known as "haiku" which captures the magic of a present moment.

**Drops of dew
washing away
world weariness.**

Basho

Below: From a series called *Mountain and Sea* by the Japanese artist Utagawa Hiroshige (1797–1858).

PLOP!

When Master Basho's most famous haiku poem came to him he became instantly enlightened. Basho was a very serious student of Zen and well educated in the scriptures. One day his master said, "I've heard you quote so much of other people's wisdom, give me one word of your own." Basho was speechless. He didn't know what to say. His mind just seized up. Suddenly the silence was broken by a gentle splash from the monastery garden. Basho spontaneously exclaimed:

"Peaceful pond
A frog jumps
Plop!"

His master laughed out loud and announced, "At last. These are the words of your true self."

Conscious Ordinariness

If you love the sacred and despise
the ordinary,
you are still bobbing in the ocean
of delusion.

Linji

Zen is nothing special. It is
living our everyday lives as an
extraordinary adventure of
spiritual awakening. It is doing
what we do, but doing it with
full awareness. Zen is not
about introducing spirituality
into our lives. It is recognizing
the miracle of the lives we are
already living.

Those who are content to be nothing
special are noble people. Don't strive.
Be ordinary. Buddhism has no room
for special effort. Eat and drink, then
move your bowels and pass water,
and when you're tired go to sleep.
Fools will find me ridiculous, but the
wise will understand.

Linji

When hungry eat,
when tired sleep.

Zen Saying

What is Zen? Ordinary mind is very Zen.
But as soon as you try to make it
something special you miss it.

Nan-ch'uan

What's the Fuss?

I haven't got any Buddhism.
I live by letting things happen.

Dogen

made

Zen is unconditional acceptance of What-is. Zen is not being attached to things going one way or going in another direction. Zen is following the flow of the river of life and allowing things to go their own way. Zen is letting things happen naturally. Zen is not a way of living your life. Zen is letting life live you.

AH SO!

A pregnant young girl claimed that Master Hakuin was the father of her illegitimate baby. The angry villagers presented Hakuin with the child and told him he must look after it. Hakuin replied, "Ah so" and took in the child and cared for it. A year later the girl confessed she had been lying and the ashamed villagers asked Hakuin for the child back. Hakuin replied, "Ah so" and gave up the child.

Right: **Golden Rock Pagoda, part of the monastery at Kyak-hi-yo, Myanmar, Japan.**

DON'T YOU KNOW WHO I AM?

The armies of a conquering tyrant were laying waste to the country when they arrived at a small village. All the inhabitants had taken refuge in the surrounding hills, except for one old monk. The tyrant was enraged at the fearlessness of the monk and personally stormed into the monastery, bellowing, "Don't you know who I am? I could draw my sword and cut you in two and not blink an eye." The monk smiled serenely and quietly replied, "Don't you know who I am? I could stand here while you draw your sword and cut me in two, and not blink an eye."

LAST WORDS

A dying master was being hassled by a student to write a final Zen poem before passing away, as was expected of him by tradition. By way of explaining his reluctance he scrawled:

> *Life is thus,*
> *Death is thus,*
> *Verse or no verse,*
> *What's the fuss?*

Left: The Zen figure Ge Changgeng sitting on his three-legged toad.

A Zen shrine on a mountain-top giving a different perspective of the world below.

Crazy Wisdom

**Zen is no
nonsense craziness.**

Alan Watts

Zen masters are renowned for their bizarre behavior. But although the Zen masters may seem irrational, Zen obeys its own logic. Their aberrant actions graphically illustrate Zen teachings in a way that words cannot. Their eccentricities exemplify a way of being that is spontaneous and unconditioned.

TOO FULL ALREADY

A famous intellectual visited a master to learn about Zen. While serving him tea the master kept on pouring after the cup was full, spilling tea everywhere. The intellectual was horrified, exclaiming, "Stop! Stop!" The master smiled and said, "The cup is full and can take no more tea unless I first empty it. In the same way your mind is full of ideas and before I can teach you Zen you must first empty it."

Above: **A Chinese soapstone figure of the founder of Zen – Bodhidharma.**

Above:
The Japanese tea
ceremony, known
as *sado* – the way
of tea – has a Zen
approach.

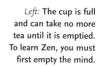

Left: The cup is full
and can take no more
tea until it is emptied.
To learn Zen, you must
first empty the mind.

SPONTANEITY

Confronted with the incomprehensible actions of a zany Zen master, the student is surprised and confounded. He doesn't know what is expected of him. His habitual reactions are inadequate to the craziness of the situation and he is forced to respond spontaneously to the present moment from his deeper being. The master has exploded the prison of his preconditioned responses to life and given him a precious taste of freedom.

HEAVEN AND HELL

A Samurai warrior asked Master Hakuin to tell him about hell and heaven. The master took one look at the Samurai and started to insult him, saying, "You are such a scruffy-looking warrior you would never understand anything." The furious Samurai pulled out his sword. "There!" said Hakuin, "This is hell." The Samurai had a flash of illumination and was overcome with gratitude, humbly bowing before the master. "There!" said Hakuin, "This is heaven."

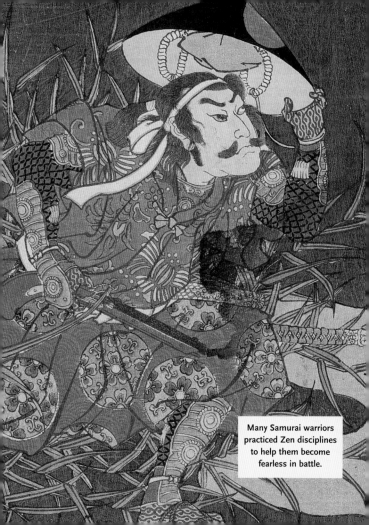

Many Samurai warriors practiced Zen disciplines to help them become fearless in battle.

Subverting the Sacred

> The Buddha is not the
> great goal of those
> that follow the Way.
> Personally, I see him
> as a privy hole.
>
> *Lin-chi*

Zen is subversive of anything that endorses the illusion of separateness. This includes the ideas that there are certain "someones" who are enlightened. Or that there are particular books that are holy. Or that there are special places that are sacred. All is One. Everything is equally sacred so nothing is particularly sacred.

BURNING THE BUDDHA

While staying at a shrine, Master Tan-hsia was feeling cold, so he took a wooden statue of the Buddha off the altar and threw it into the fire. The keeper of the shrine was dismayed and angry. In response, the Master began looking among the ashes. "What are you

Left: A golden statue of the Buddha from Zorge Monastery Temple, Sichuan province, China.

doing?" inquired the keeper of the shrine. "Looking for holy relics in the ashes," replied the master. "You won't find them in the ashes of a wooden statue," said the keeper. "If that is so," the master concluded, "can I have another couple of Buddhas for the fire to keep me warm?"

EVERYWHERE IS HOLY

A sixteen-year-old girl became enlightened after studying with Master Hakuin. One day her father found her in meditation while sitting on a box. "What are you doing?" he exclaimed, "There is a statue of the Buddha in that box." The young girl replied to her astonished father, "If there is any place where the Buddha does not exist — take me there!"

BUDDHA-BASHING

Zen masters are infamous for their irreverence. They call each other "brainless," the holy scriptures "waste paper," and Buddhism "a disease." Zen paintings portray great masters as ridiculous and comical. In this way they prevent their students from idolizing anyone as an enlightened being and help them realize that they must seek the enlightened being within themselves.

OLD RICE-BAGS

Frequently the Zen masters referred to each other as "old rice bags" and with other uncomplimentary terms, not out of professional jealousy, but because it amused them to think that they and their wise brothers were supposed by ordinary standards to be so especially holy. They realized that everything was holy, even cooking pots and odd leaves blown about by the wind, and that there was nothing particularly venerable about themselves.

Alan Watts

COMMENTS ON THE FOUNDER OF ZEN

That broken-toothed old Hindu, Bodhidharma, came thousands of miles over the sea from India to China as if he had something wonderful. He is like raising waves without wind. After he remained years in China he had only one disciple and that one had lost his arm and was deformed. Alas, ever since he has had brainless disciples. Why did Bodhidharma come to China? For years monks have discussed this. All the troubles that have followed since came from that teacher and disciple.

Master Mummon

Zazen

**Find the silence
which contains thoughts.**

Hakuin

The name "Zen" is a Japanese
adaptation of the Chinese name
"Ch'an" which in turn comes from
the Sanskrit word "Dhyana,"
meaning "meditation." Meditation,
known as *zazen*, or simply "sitting," is the central spiritual
practice in Zen Buddhism. Meditation is a technique for becoming
aware of awareness itself.

**If you walk, just walk.
If you sit, just sit.
But don't wobble.**

Yunmen

Right: Meditation is known
as *zazen*, which means
sitting, and is central to Zen
Buddhist spiritual practices.

CLEAR CONSCIOUSNESS

In meditation, practitioners sit perfectly still and allow their thoughts to come to a rest. Just as a puddle of muddy water slowly clears when left undisturbed, so the mind clears of thought when we stop agitating it by paying attention to the constant chatter in our heads. Through meditation it is possible to become conscious of the empty space within which thoughts rise and fall. This is our true identity.

Meditation is the reservoir of wisdom.

Chi-sha Daishi

A LIFE AND
DEATH SITUATION

The inner peace sought by Zen meditators is not the comforting dullness of sleep, but the super-awakeness of being completely present. Sometimes the alertness necessary is compared to that of someone facing a life and death situation. Or to having the most fascinating thought you've ever had – only without the thought!

Right: **Imagine hanging from a cliff face and you will know the alertness of Zen mind.**

THIS IS MEDITATION

Outwardly in the world of good and
evil, yet without thoughts stirring
the heart — this is meditation.

Inwardly seeing one's own true
nature and not being distracted
from it — this is meditation.

Hui-neng

Right: The test of Zen is finding the still center within, even during the most hectic times of our lives.

If you have been practicing silent meditation but when you are in the midst of activity your mind is still not calm and free, this means you have not gained anything from your silent meditation.

Dahui

STILL CENTER WITHIN

Zen is not about becoming an expert meditator who can sit cross-legged for hours at a time. Zen is about finding the still center of consciousness within at all times. By limiting sensual stimulation, meditation makes it easier to do this. But the real test is also finding this still center when we reenter the maelstrom of our busy lives.

DUMB LUMPS

The ancients saw how helpless people were and suggested they silently meditated. This was wise advice. But later on people didn't understand what the ancients had meant. They just closed their eyes, suppressed body and mind, and sat like a lump waiting for enlightenment. How dumb can you get?!

Foyan

Heaven and hell are in the mind.
When the mind is always empty, you journey
from place to place in the country of the
Buddhas. When the mind is always moving,
you travel from one hell to the next hell.

Bodhidharma

Unanswerable Questions

What was your original face before your parents were born?

Zen Koan

Some schools of Zen practice meditation by contemplating "koans." A koan is a kind of Zen riddle. These seemingly illogical questions cannot be solved with the powers of the rational mind — only through a flash of intuitive insight. They are not answered by words but by a transformation of consciousness.

SPONTANEOUS INSIGHT

Contemplating a koan sets up a deep tension in the logical mind of the student until a sudden call of a bird, a flash of lightning, a blow from a stick, or anything at all, triggers a spontaneous awakening. Until this happens the master will reject all the student's answers to the koan, no matter how philosophically erudite. When this expansion of consciousness occurs, any answer that the student may give will be the right answer — even something that is completely absurd.

What is the sound of one hand clapping?

Zen Koan

If all things return to the One, where does the One return to?

Zen Koan

MU!

Master Ekai meditated on a koan for six years, until one day he heard the monastery drum and was spontaneously enlightened. This koan was the exclamation "Mu!," which literally means "Not!" Ekai would often simply shout "Mu!" in reply to his students' questions as a way of pointing to an answer beyond the logical mind. "Mu!" declares "Anything you can think is not the answer." "Mu!" demands "Abandon your question and directly experience What-is."

> True meditation is making everything — coughing, swallowing, waving, movement and stillness, speaking and acting, good and evil, fame and shame, loss and gain, right and wrong — into one single koan.
>
> *Hakuin*

Below: A Zen monastery resonates with the sound of a drum.

When "Mu!" bears fruit, quite
spontaneously inside and out will become
One. You will end up like a dumb man
who has awoken from dreaming. You will
know yourself – but only for yourself.
"Mu!" will suddenly explode, shaking the
earth and opening the heavens.

Ekai

Mission Impossible

When you try to stop doing to achieve being,
this very effort fills you with doing.

Seng-t'san

Zen encourages us to undergo strenuous spiritual practices to help us see through the illusion of separateness and experience enlightenment. Yet it also teaches that enlightenment can actually only occur spontaneously, and believing we are doing something, even spiritual practices, only endorses the false idea of the ego.

THE ZEN DILEMMA
We are caught in a "Catch 22" situation. We need to free ourselves from the illusion of being a separate self. What can we do? The idea that there is a "someone" to do anything about the problem is the problem itself! Does Zen have a solution for this impossible dilemma? Mu!

If you want to find Zen,
begin by not looking for it.
Anything you find
*   through thinking*
is already a product of the mind.

Yuanwu

MEDITATION DOESN'T WORK

One day Master Huai Jang asked a student who was practicing meditation, "What are you doing?" The student replied, "Trying to be a Buddha." Huai Jang picked up a stone and began rubbing it. "What are you doing?" asked the student. Huai Jang answered, "I am trying to make a mirror." The astonished student told him, "No amount of polishing will make a stone a mirror." Huai Jang commented wryly, "No amount of meditation will make you a Buddha."

DREAMING THAT YOU'VE WOKEN UP

Trying to get rid of habitual states of mind without having seen into your own nature is like trying to get rid of a dream while asleep. The desire to dispel the dream is just part of the dream. Knowing that it is a dream is also just part of the dream. It doesn't matter how much you search for something in a dream, you will never find it.

Bassui

Left: The straight back of a Zen monk in meditation.

made easy

ALREADY PERFECT

Hoping to gain spiritual merit,
people perform a vast number
of complex practices as countless
as the grains of sand on the
riverbed of the Ganges; but you
are essentially already perfect in
every way. Don't try to augment
perfection with meaningless
practice. If it's the right occasion
to perform them, let practices
happen. When the time has
passed, let them stop. If you
are not absolutely sure that
mind is the Buddha, and if you
are attached to the ideas of
winning merit from spiritual
practices, then your thinking is
misguided and not in harmony
with the Way. To practice complex
spiritual practices is to progress
step by step; but the eternal
Buddha is not a Buddha of
progressive stages. Just awaken
to the one Mind, and there is
absolutely nothing to be attained.
This is the real Buddha.

Huang-po

made
easy

Below: Varanasi on the holy
River Ganges in an important
Hindu place of pilgrimage.

Don't Be a Buddhist

Don't be a Buddhist.
The secret is in you.

Foyan

You do not have to become a Buddhist to understand Zen. In fact to do so would be a fatal error. Seeing yourself as a "Buddhist" or a "Zen practitioner" may sound exotic and impressive, but it is actually just adding another layer to the illusion of self. Don't become anything. Be what you are. This is the message of Zen.

NO SELF

Zen is not about changing into a spiritual person. Zen is realizing the eternal truth of "no self." Zen is about transcending all the labels and definitions we append to ourselves and directly experiencing the ineffable Buddha-nature. Zen is being a conscious witness of the unfolding miracle of

Right: **To find the Buddha within, don't be a Buddhist – be yourself.**

existence, in all its unified diversity, familiar strangeness, and miraculous ordinariness.

DISCOVERING YOUR ESSENTIAL NATURE

No one can teach you Zen. Zen is about discovering your essential nature for yourself. This is a personal journey to transcend your personality and discover the Buddha-nature that is your true identity. Enlightenment is not just for holy people. Your essential nature is no different from that of the Buddha. We are all sleepers waiting to awaken from the dream of separateness.

It is nonsense to insist that we cannot achieve enlightenment without learned and pious teachers. Because wisdom is innate, we can all enlighten ourselves.

Hui-neng

There is nothing lacking in you.
You are no different from the Buddha.

Tao-hsin

All the various teachings and practices of Zen are only to encourage you to individually look back into yourself and discover your original mind, so that you may know your essential nature and rest in a state of great peace and happiness.

Yuansou

Index